FINDING DINOSAURS
IGUANODON

by Rebecca E. Hirsch

FOCUS READERS

WWW.FOCUSREADERS.COM

Focus Readers is distributed by North Star Editions:
sales@northstareditions.com | 888-417-0195

Produced for Focus Readers by Red Line Editorial.

Content Consultant: Dr. David B. Weishampel, Professor Emeritus, Center for Functional Anatomy and Evolution, Johns Hopkins University School of Medicine

Photographs ©: Elenarts/Shutterstock Images, cover, 1; Paul D. Stewart/Science Source, 4–5; The Natural History Museum/Alamy, 7, 15, 17 (top); World History Archive/Newscom, 9; Oxford Science Archive/Heritage Images/Glow Images, 11; Alice Turner/Stocktrek Images/Science Source, 12–13; ilbusca/iStockphoto, 17 (middle); leonello/iStockphoto, 17 (bottom); Elenarts/iStockphoto, 18; Corey Ford/iStockphoto, 20–21; Sergey Krasovskiy/Stocktrek Images, Inc./Alamy, 23; Wild Doc/iStockphoto, 24; Alizada Studios/Shutterstock Images, 26–27; Nikreates/Alamy, 29

ISBN
978-1-63517-504-2 (hardcover)
978-1-63517-576-9 (paperback)
978-1-63517-720-6 (ebook pdf)
978-1-63517-648-3 (hosted ebook)

Library of Congress Control Number: 2017948064

Printed in the United States of America
Mankato, MN
November, 2017

ABOUT THE AUTHOR

Rebecca E. Hirsch is a PhD-trained scientist and the award-winning author of dozens of books about science for children. She lives in Pennsylvania with her family and assorted pets.

TABLE OF CONTENTS

Pl III

CHAPTER 1

LIKE A LIZARD

In the 1820s, Gideon Mantell came upon some curious fossils. Mantell was an English doctor and amateur fossil hunter. How he got the fossils is a bit of a mystery. His wife, Mary Ann, might have found the fossils beside a road. Or, local workers might have found the fossils in a quarry and brought them to Mantell.

Mantell wrote this letter soon after receiving the fossils.

But no matter how he got them, the fossils helped Mantell make an important discovery.

The fossils looked like huge teeth. Some were 5 inches (13 cm) long. The teeth had a flat, worn shape. That shape meant the teeth had come from an **herbivore**.

Mantell asked other scientists to help identify what animal the teeth came from. One scientist thought the teeth were from a large fish. Another suggested a rhinoceros. Mantell was not convinced. He took the teeth to a museum in London. This museum had **specimens** from all known animal species. Mantell searched

This is one of the Iguanodon teeth the Mantells discovered.

through the specimens. But he did not find a match for the teeth.

At the museum, a young scientist named Samuel Stutchbury took a look at the fossils. Stutchbury was an expert on iguanas. He showed Mantell some iguana teeth. The iguana teeth were much smaller than the fossil teeth. But they had the same shape.

Mantell concluded that the teeth had come from a giant plant-eating lizard. He named this lizard *Iguanodon*, which means "iguana tooth." Mantell believed these giant reptiles had once lived on Earth. But they were now **extinct**.

Many scientists did not agree with him. Then other people began finding

NAMING DINOSAURS

In 1842, scientist Richard Owen invented the word *dinosaur*. This word means "terrible lizard" or "terribly great lizard." Owen based this new group on three animals: Iguanodon, a **carnivore** called Megalosaurus, and an herbivore called Hylaeosaurus. Today, both lizards and dinosaurs are considered members of the reptile family.

This cast of an Iguanodon skull shows the shape of its teeth and jaws.

more fossils of large reptiles. Eventually, scientists came to agree that giant reptiles had once roamed the earth.

THE BERNISSART SKELETONS

In 1878, two coal miners in Bernissart, Belgium, discovered a clay-filled crack filled with fossils. The find included more than 30 Iguanodon fossils. Earlier Iguanodon finds had been of small, disconnected bones or scattered remains. But these were skeletons of complete dinosaurs.

The skeletons were from two different species. The first was the same species Mantell had studied. The second was a new, larger species. It was called *Iguanodon bernissartensis*. The fossils also included remains of fish, reptiles, and plants. These fossils gave scientists information about the world in which Iguanodon lived.

The mine was closed for two years while people worked to **excavate** the fossils. They coated the fossils in wet paper, clay, and plaster

Miners lifted the fossils out of a crack in the clay.

for protection. Then they brought them to the
surface. The skeletons are now on display at the
Royal Belgian Institute of Natural Sciences in
Brussels, Belgium.

CHAPTER 2

GIANT GRAZERS

Iguanodon was a large, lumbering animal. It had sturdy legs and a big, heavy tail. Its body was 33 to 36 feet (10 to 11 m) long. It weighed more than 5,500 pounds (2,500 kg). That is as much as an Asian elephant.

Iguanodon had a hard, turtle-like beak that covered the front of its jaws.

Iguanodon may have clipped twigs off trees with its sharp beak.

Iguanodon had no teeth at the front of its mouth. But its back jaws were lined with tough teeth for grinding. The teeth were diamond shaped. They had ridges along the sides. They likely wore down with use over time.

Iguanodon's hands had five fingers. One finger was opposable. It could bend across the hand and touch the other fingers. The dinosaur likely used this

IGUANODON DIET

Iguanodon may have eaten horsetail plants and tree leaves. First, it used its sharp beak to clip off the food. Then it chewed the food with its powerful jaws. It likely moved its upper jaw in a sideways motion.

This fossilized Iguanodon hand shows the animal's large thumb spike.

finger to grasp plants. The middle three fingers had a thick covering of horn. These fingers could have supported the dinosaur's weight as it walked.

Iguanodon's thumb stuck out to the side. It had a long, sharp spike on the end.

This spike could be up to 12 inches (30 cm) long. Iguanodon probably used its spiked thumb for fighting. It may have also used the spike to rake branches of trees down to its mouth.

At first, **paleontologists** thought the spike was on Iguanodon's nose. But they later discovered that was wrong. They found more complete skeletons. They also found a thumb with the spike attached.

Scientists changed their minds about how Iguanodon stood, too. At first, scientists believed Iguanodon stood on four legs like a lizard. Later scientists found skeletons which showed that the dinosaur's front legs were shorter.

RECONSTRUCTING IGUANODON

1. The first reconstructions showed Iguanodon standing on four legs like a lizard, with a spike on its nose.

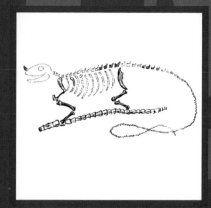

2. Later reconstructions showed Iguanodon on two legs, with its tail on the ground for support.

3. Modern reconstructions show the animal with its tail held out straight from the body.

Iguanodon may have sometimes stood on two legs.

As a result, scientists believed Iguanodon stood on only two legs. They thought its heavy tail rested on the ground, like a kangaroo's tail. Then more intact skeletons were found. They showed that the tail was held out in a straight line.

Iguanodon's short arms suggested the dinosaur could walk on two legs. But Iguanodon also had hoofed fingers and strong bones in its arms and shoulders. These traits suggest that the dinosaur used its hands for walking at least some of the time. Modern scientists think Iguanodon may have walked on all fours while it grazed. But it would have been able to use just two legs at other times.

CHAPTER 3

EARLY CRETACEOUS LIFE

Iguanodon lived 100 million years ago during the Early Cretaceous period. At this time, dinosaurs roamed forests full of **conifers**, **cycads**, and ferns. **Pterosaurs** flew in the skies. Small, furry mammals hid in the bushes.

The world was warmer during the Early Cretaceous period than it is today.

Iguanodon was probably common in marshy areas.

The sea level was higher, too. Shallow seas covered large areas of land.

Iguanodon lived in wetlands across Europe. Remains have been found from Britain, Portugal, and Spain in the west to the Ural Mountains in the east.

Other plant-eating dinosaurs lived alongside Iguanodon. These included the armored Polacanthus and the small, speedy Hypsilophodon. Iguanodon's main **predator** was called Neovenator. This sleek and streamlined dinosaur could be up to 33 feet (10 m) long.

Young Iguanodons might have been fast enough to outrun predators. But adults were likely too slow and heavy.

Neovenator (back) would have also eaten Polacanthus.

Studying dinosaur tracks helps scientists learn how these ancient animals may have lived.

Instead, adults would have turned and faced the predator. They might have reared up on their hind legs and swiped at the predator's head with their massive thumb spikes.

There is some evidence that Iguanodon lived in herds. Footprint tracks found in England seem to show several Iguanodons moving together in the same direction. In addition, a large number of Iguanodon remains were discovered in one place in Germany. It appears that these animals drowned in a flash flood.

SAFETY IN NUMBERS

Living in herds would have given herbivores such as Iguanodon better protection from predators. If Iguanodon did live in herds, very young or old animals might have been kept near the center of the herd. Large, healthy adults would have patrolled the outside. This would help protect the weaker animals.

CHAPTER 4

CURRENT QUESTIONS

Iguanodon disappeared approximately 100 million years ago, during the Early Cretaceous period. But many other dinosaurs survived until the end of the Cretaceous period. This was millions of years after Iguanodon died out. Scientists do not know why Iguanodon went extinct so much earlier than other dinosaurs.

Iguanodon (left) was smaller than the dinosaur Diplodocus (right).

They do know that as Iguanodon disappeared, the number of hadrosaurids grew. These duck-billed dinosaurs were close relatives of Iguanodon. The hadrosaurids became the most common plant-eaters by the end of the age of the dinosaurs. Their increasing population may have caused Iguanodon to die out.

Iguanodon was one of the first dinosaurs ever discovered. It remains one of the most well-known. Yet scientists still have many questions about it. They do not know exactly which plants it ate. They are not certain if it lived in herds. And they are not sure how often it walked on two legs instead of four.

The Dinosaur Isle Museum in the United Kingdom contains this Iguanodon skeleton.

As fossil hunters continue to make discoveries, their findings will open the way for answers about these giant herbivores.

FOCUS ON
IGUANODON

Write your answers on a separate piece of paper.

1. Write a paragraph describing the habitat in which Iguanodon lived.

2. Would it be easier for young Iguanodons or adult Iguanodons to defend themselves against predators? Why?

3. What part of an Iguanodon's hand might have been used for walking on all fours?

    A. the thumb spike

    B. the hoofed middle fingers

    C. the opposable fifth finger

4. What could have been the relationship between Iguanodon and the hadrosaurids?

    A. Iguanodon and the hadrosaurids might have competed for the same food.

    B. The hadrosaurids might have hunted and eaten Iguanodon.

    C. Iguanodon might have descended from the hadrosaurids.

Answer key on page 32.

GLOSSARY

carnivore
An animal that eats meat.

conifers
Trees that have needle-shaped leaves and produce cones.

cycads
Trees with thick trunks and leathery, palm-like leaves.

excavate
To remove something from the ground by digging.

extinct
No longer living on Earth.

herbivore
An animal that eats only plants.

paleontologists
Scientists who study the ancient past and the fossil remains of ancient living things.

predator
An animal that hunts other animals for food.

pterosaurs
Ancient animals that had featherless wings and could fly.

specimens
The remains of individual animals that show what the entire group of animals was like.

TO LEARN MORE

BOOKS

Alonso, Juan Carlos, and Gregory S. Paul. *The Early Cretaceous: Notes, Drawings, and Observations from Prehistory.* Lake Forest, CA: Walter Foster Jr., 2015.

Gray, Susan H. *Iguanodon.* Mankato, MN: The Child's World, 2015.

Thimmesh, Catherine. *Scaly Spotted Feathered Frilled: How Do We Know What Dinosaurs Really Looked Like?* Boston: Houghton Mifflin Harcourt, 2013.

NOTE TO EDUCATORS

Visit **www.focusreaders.com** to find lesson plans, activities, links, and other resources related to this title.

INDEX